THE OUTER BAY

The sea is as close as
we come to another world.
–Anne Stevenson

Beyond the tidal pools and kelp forests, beyond the

shallow waters pressed close against the shores, lies another world.

Sixty miles offshore, the outer reaches of Monterey Bay

blend into the world of the open ocean.

The far reaches of sunlit ocean wrap our planet in their

blue embrace. Below lies the dark vastness of the deep sea. These

restless waters are home to translucent, pulsing jellies and sleek,

muscular fishes; pastures of microscopic plants and huge whales.

The Monterey Bay Aquarium's Outer Bay wing

is a window onto the endless, mysterious ocean world that lies

beyond the narrow strand of coastal habitats.

Come closer and see.

MONTEREY BAY AQUARIUM

WHAT IS THE OUTER BAY?

It takes only minutes to make your way from the aquarium entrance to the Outer Bay exhibits. But as you gaze at the school of anchovies swirling overhead in silvery welcome, know that you've traveled sixty miles offshore.

A journey to the outer bay carries you further than can be measured in miles. The seafloor drops away, at first gradually, then plunging two miles below the surface. Land's influence ebbs, and you enter the pelagic realm—ruled by water alone.

Gone are the hard edges and solid footing offered by rocky reefs, the sheltering structure of the kelp forests. Here, amid featureless water, the only visible boundary is the sea's surface.

But the creatures at home here are attuned to more subtle boundaries. Their world is organized by light, temperature, salinity and the intricate interactions among the inhabitants themselves.

Tunas are the nomads of tropical and temperate oceans. These long-distance migrators can swim up to 100 miles a day; some may travel 10,000 miles in a year.

Boundaries almost unnoticeable to us are vitally real to those who live here. One patch of water may teem with life, while another nearby lies nearly barren. The plants and animals of the Outer Bay exhibits are at home near the surface where sunlight powers a profusion of life. Below a few hundred feet, light fades into the deep sea darkness of a huge submarine canyon where life is more scarce and scattered.

In this blue world of wide-open spaces, creatures never come to rest. Whether they swim or drift, they live their lives on the move.

The restless, sunlit waters sixty miles offshore... our journey takes us there. But it also takes us further.

A visit to the Outer Bay carries us to the edge of another world.

DRIFTERS

In the stories of life in the outer bay, the starring roles belong to some of the smallest creatures, the ocean's drifters—the plankton. Tremendous in number, myriad plants and animals flow with the currents.

The outer bay is a world of these drifters: one-celled plants, predatory jellies, the larvae of crabs, sea stars and fishes, swarms of copepods and shrimplike krill. At times the water here teems with billions and billions, floating in shifting clouds.

In their multitude and diversity, they make up vital, complex communities in open waters.

From the spot prawns patrolling the seafloor to the barnacles carpeting rocky tidepools, from the great blue whales plying the ocean's far reaches to the tiny Arctic terns on their pole-to-pole migrations, nearly all life in the ocean owes its being to the plankton.

Snowflake-shaped larval jellies and predatory sea gooseberries are among the myriad tiny dirfters in the outer bay.

Like other barnacles, pelagic barnacles live cemented to solid objects—but the objects they're attached to float free in the sea.

Many plankton spend only part of their lives in open water. As adults, some become swimmers; others settle down to life on the seafloor.

Larval crabs drift for many weeks, then settle down and change into their adult forms.

The plankton lab features microscopes for exploring samples of living plankton and a changing display of seasonally abundant plankton.

This comb jelly can eat gelatinous animals larger than itself by biting off pieces using special toothlike structures in its mouth.

The entire life cycle of the purple-striped jelly was first described by researchers here at the Monterey Bay Aquarium.

A transparent, torpedo-shaped arrowworm dominates this sample of plankton from the bay. Arrowworms are fearsome predators of copepods and other animal plankton.

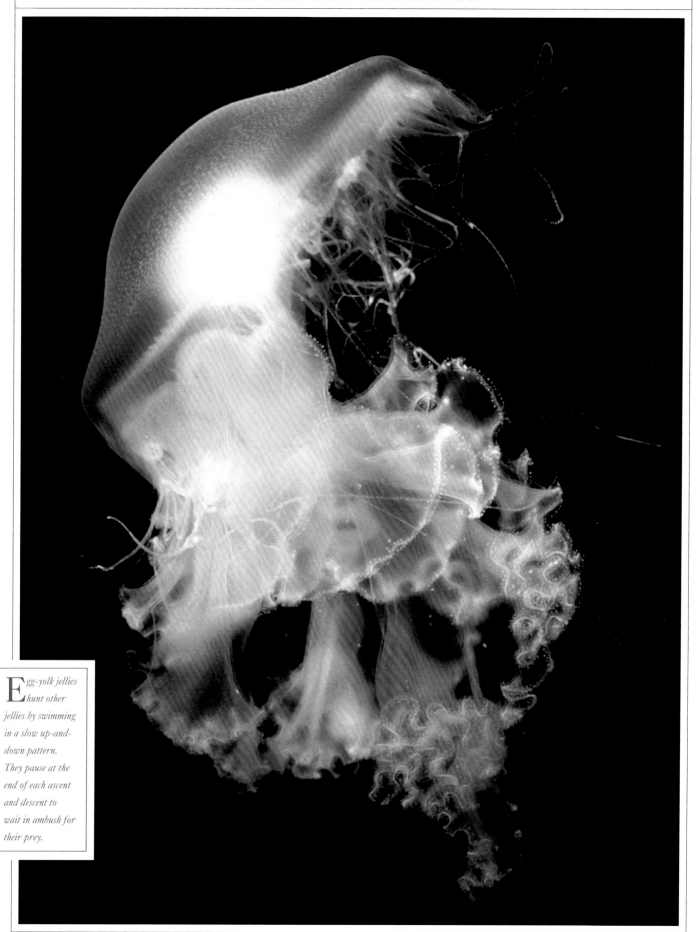

Egg-yolk jellies hunt other jellies by swimming in a slow up-and-down pattern. They pause at the end of each ascent and descent to wait in ambush for their prey.

At times, diatoms drift by the billions in the outer bay. The abundance of these microscopic plants here is one reason for the rich marine life along our coast.

Life Sciences staff will provide fresh samples of plankton every day for the plankton lab.

Krill are the favorite food of blue whales. A single whale may eat a ton—that is 18 million krill—at every meal.

In spring and summer, micro-scopic plants grow in such numbers they turn outer bay water green.

Scanning the surface waters of the outer bay, you won't see much life–a few soaring birds, perhaps a whale's spout. Under water, you might see translucent jellies drifting by or a school of squid or fish; large animals are only an occasional sight here.

But there's more to outer bay life than large animals.

The outer bay's full of tiny drifters: plants and animals too small to see without a microscope.

Some spend their whole lives drifting with the currents. For others, drifting is just a phase. Sea stars, crabs, fishes and others drift as larvae, then settle down or grow up to become swimmers as adults.

In open waters, life begins with nourishing pastures of one-celled plants. Where conditions are right–enough light, enough nutrients–marine life flourishes. Where light or nutrients are lacking, the ocean lies as blue and barren as an empty sky.

Conditions are right along our coast, as in few other places, and plant plankton flourish. In spring and summer they color the water a murky golden brown by their sheer numbers.

Hordes of tiny drifting animals graze on the plants. Clouds of copepods, squadrons of gelatinous, soft-bodied salps reap the harvest, their populations exploding as they feast on the bounty of these watery pastures.

As these grazers multiply, they spur the growth of voracious predators: darting arrowworms, delicate, but deadly, sea gooseberries and a host of others.

All live together in a fierce microcosm.

Tiny drifters are the sea's biggest story. One that's told bigger than life in the Outer Bay galleries.

Here, you can look through microscopes at fantastic larval forms and follow volunteers on tours through miniature seascapes.

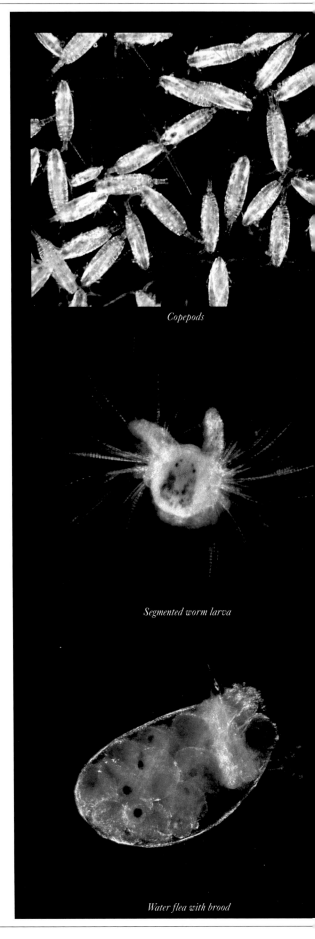

Copepods

Segmented worm larva

Water flea with brood

Purple-striped jelly larva

Crab larva

Copepod

Sea gooseberry

Moon jelly larva

Crab larvae

By-the-wind sailors drift in open waters. But spring winds sometimes blow them into the bay.

Jellies can be very sensitive to water quality. Changes in the health of jelly populations may be a warning of larger environmental problems.

The Monterey Bay Aquarium Research Institute's ROV is equipped with tools that allow scientists to collect jellies alive for study at the aquarium.

Jellies in the Outer Bay exhibits consume many gallons of brine shrimp each day.

All head and no tail, ocean sunfish look like big leathery frisbees. They scull along by flapping their top and bottom fins, while using their stumpy tail to steer.

A set of sharp teeth help make California barracudas terrific predators on small fishes.

Brown pelicans are one of the many animals which visit the outer bay seasonally to feast on the bounty of fishes and other marine life here.

This is the largest one-piece aquarium window in the world! It measures 56 1/2-feet long, 17-feet tall and 12 3/4-inches thick. It weighs nearly 39 tons.

Thresher sharks patrol open waters hunting for the schools of mackerel and other fishes they eat.

In contrast to the incredible diversity and number of the ocean's drifters, the swimmers are few in number and fewer in kind. But for most of us, these animals–powerful sharks, great whales, dense schools of silvery fishes, mysterious squid and soaring seabirds–embody the spirit of life in the outer bay.

The freedom of their seemingly endless travels captures our imaginations. We take to the seas to hunt them using hooks, nets and harpoons. Because they're larger and more like us–animals with backbones–they're more familiar to us than are the hordes of alien-looking plankton. But in spite of the common bonds we share, these are still creatures of that other world, the ocean world offshore.

Above all else, the nekton are built to travel. Sleek and powerful, tireless and efficient, they traverse the far reaches of the oceans. Many are on the go from the moment they're born until the time they die. For them, to stop would be to suffocate or to sink into the depths. But while they travel ceaselessly, they don't travel randomly. They, like the drifters, are tied to the ocean's structure: temperature, salinity, currents.

The shifting edges of several great ocean water masses overlap in the outer bay, and each carries its own group of swimmers to enrich these waters. Salmon migrate from streams here to colder waters to the north. Tuna follow the great currents that cross the central Pacific. In late summer, tropical sea turtles and ocean sunfish follow tongues of warm water north into the bay. Some animals migrate more widely. Gray whales journey north to subarctic waters in summer, then back to the subtropical waters off Baja California in winter. Red phalarope

Green sea turtles live in the tropics, but sometimes follow warm currents north to the outer bay.

Open ocean fishes cross national boundaries and wise management of their stocks requires international cooperation.

Schools of silvery anchovies feed on the abundance of plankton in the outer bay.

A colorful cutout of a humpback whale in the Flippers, Flukes & Fun exhibit introduces children to the lives of marine mammals.

The outer bay is an important point in the migration routes of birds, marine mammals and fishes. Some, like tuna, circle the Pacific; others, like Arctic terns, fly from pole to pole.

The aquarium's Outer Bay galleries represent the first permanent tuna exhibit in the United States.

The ribs of the giant Outer Bay exhibit now support a fiberglass liner that holds the blue tile visitors see.

The ocean sunfish doesn't need to be a fast swimmer to catch its food—it eats jellies and other slow-drifting prey.

We customize the feeding of each kind of fish in the exhibit to ensure that everyone gets enough.

fly from the Arctic to the tip of South America on their migrations.

Fish, bird or mammal, the restless movements of all these travelers are driven by two vital needs: the search for food to fuel their high-energy lifestyles and the irrepressible urge to reach suitable spawning areas where their young can find the special conditions they need to survive. And in the Ocean Travelers exhibit, visitors can trace their life journeys.

Gazing into the one-million gallon Outer Bay exhibit, you feel as if you've entered the world of the great ocean swimmers. Strange ocean sunfish, big as doors, flap lazily by a huge window that seems to open directly onto the ocean. Schools of bonito and yellowfin tuna swim into view, disappear, then re-appear from the blue depths. California barracuda swim near the surface.

Around the corner, the swimmers alcove highlights the adaptations of fishes to open water life. Interactive exhibits show how tuna slice effortlessly through water. The need for speed and efficient swimming has molded their teardrop-shaped bodies and crescent-shaped tails that provide maximum thrust. Even their colors have been painted by their environment. Most wear shades of silvery blue or green that blend into the surrounding water. And most are countershaded with dark backs and lighter bellies to make them harder to see from both above and below—vital camouflage in this wide open world.

In addition to camouflage, many open water fishes also find safety in numbers, and other interactives here explore the role of schooling as a defense. Speed and streamlining, countershading and schooling: for the restless swimmers of the outer bay, these are the keys to survival.

A blue shark swims slowly, its long pectoral fins outspread. The fins act like the wings of a glider, stabilizing the shark and giving it lift to soar through the water.

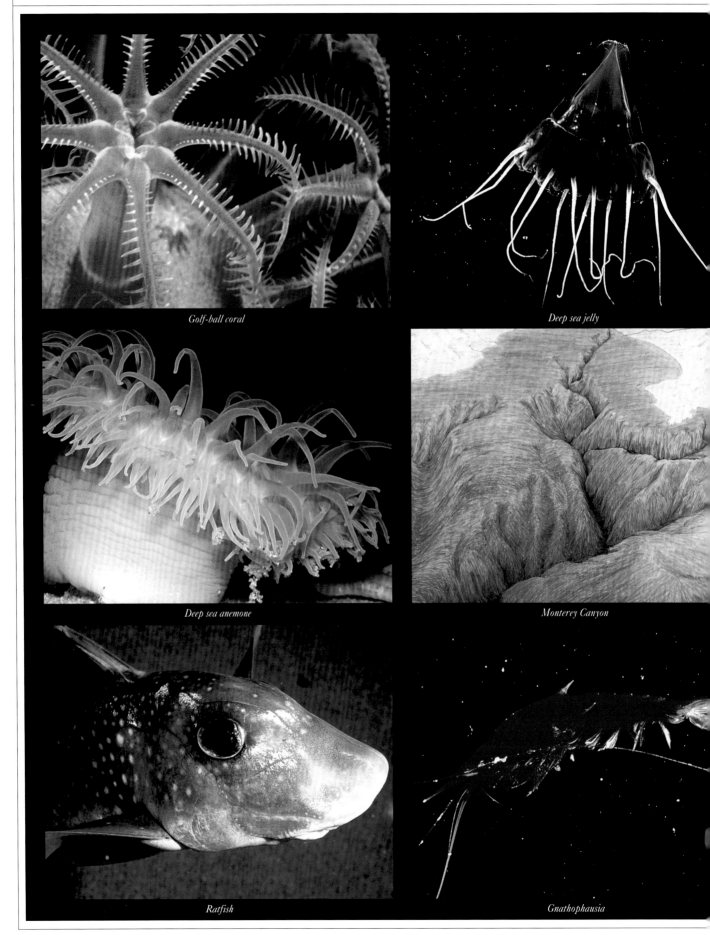

Golf-ball coral

Deep sea jelly

Deep sea anemone

Monterey Canyon

Ratfish

Gnathophausia

THE CANYON

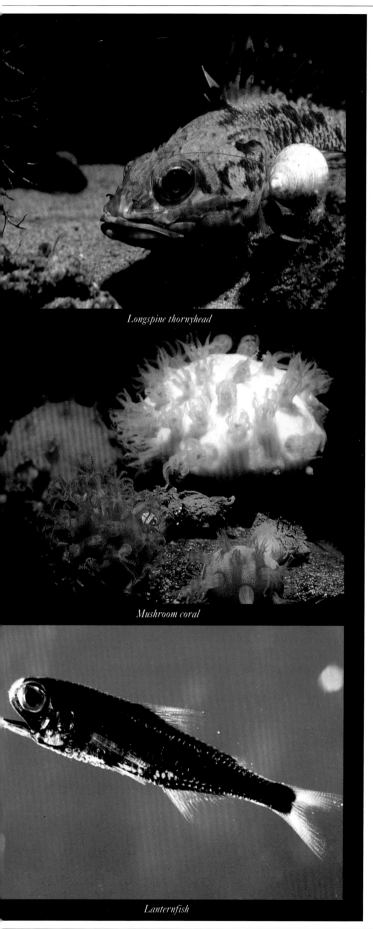

Longspine thornyhead

Mushroom coral

Lanternfish

The Monterey Bay Aquarium tells the stories of life in the bay. And the opening of the Outer Bay galleries stands as a milestone along the way.

But our offshore journey leaves us poised on the edge of a larger story. Beneath the restless surface waters lie the dark, deep sea waters of the immense Monterey submarine canyon.

The canyon rivals the Grand Canyon of the Colorado in size. From its head near Moss Landing, the canyon bends and curves as it runs out to sea. Sixty miles out and more than two miles below the surface–this is where our journey will lead next with the opening of the first floor of The Outer Bay wing.

Teams of scientists, aquarists, writers and designers are already at work weaving the story of the deep sea. Part adventure, part mystery, it's a story populated by strange and marvelous animals at home in a world as alien to us as outer space.

The opening's scheduled for the year 2000, but visitors can already get a preview.

Scientists at our sister institution, the Monterey Bay Aquarium Research Institute, are exploring the canyon's depths using remotely operated vehicles–unmanned submersibles equipped with sophisticated instruments and high-resolution video to pierce the darkness.

Aquarium visitors can join in their discoveries. Each week, live video from their missions is beamed here as part of the "Live from the Deep Canyon" program. You can come join the adventure now.

WORKING TOWARDS
OUR FUTURE

The outer bay with all its remarkable creatures may seem like

an alien world to us. But this world is a vital part

of our own. Every day, our actions affect this world. And changes there

can have profound effects on our daily lives.

What might a tuna, crossing the Pacific on the

ages-old migration routes of its ancestors, find on its journey today?

Plastic trash, polluted water, abandoned

drift nets a mile long...refuse from our rapidly growing population.

The aquarium tells the stories of life in

the bay in order to stimulate a sense of stewardship towards

the bay and the oceans beyond.

These are things we care deeply about. We encourage you to get

involved in marine conservation issues. It's up to each

of us to work to ensure that tuna continue their wondrous journeys, that

the oceans remain healthy and full of life.

The future of our planet—our future—depends on it.